The Ups and Downs of a Wall Street Trader during the Depths of the Great Depression of the 1930s

By
David Feldman

Analyst and Partner
N.Y. Stock Exchange Firm
in the 1930s and 1940s

FRASER PUBLISHING COMPANY
Burlington, Vermont

Copyright © 1997 by David Feldman

Published in 1997 by Fraser Publishing Company
                a division of Fraser Management
                Box 494
                Burlington, VT 05402

All rights reserved. No part of this book may be reproduced or transmitted in any form or by any means, electronic or mechanical, including photocopying, recording, or by any information storage and retrieval system, without permission in writing from the publisher, except in the case of brief quotations to be used in critical reviews or articles.

Library of Congress Cataloging-in-Publication Data
Feldman, David, 1911-
   The ups and downs of a Wall Street trader
   during the depths of the Great Depression
   of the 1930s / by David Feldman.
      p.   cm.
     ISBN: 0-87034-128-6 (paper)
     1. Feldman, David, 1911-   . 2. Stockbrokers—United States—Biography. 3. Depressions—1929—United States. 4. New York Stock Exchange—History.
5. Wall Street—History. I. Title.
HG4928.5.F45   1997
332.63'22'092—dc21
[B]

                                                    97-35164
                                                    CIP

Printed in the United States of America

TABLE OF CONTENTS

	PAGE
1925, And An Early Lesson in Finance	1
A Totally Different Country	5
The Bad Guys and the Good Guys	7
Games the Swindlers Played	11
A "New Era" is Upon Us!	17
1929 Highs vs. 1932 Lows	27
End of the Year 1929 Our Business Leaders Predict What is Going to Happen in 1930 and Beyond	29
So How Come a Group of Foreigners Were the Only Ones That Had it Exactly Right?	35
On Becoming a Stock Broker in the Early 1930s	37
Making Money. Easiest Thing in the World!	41
The Typical Brokerage Office of the 1930s	45
1932—Bottom of the Barrel Just Couldn't Be Worse	49
"Bring Beer Back With Frank and Jack"	57
On the Way to Becoming a Millionaire! The Loft, Incorporated, Frolic	65
And What About Today's Markets?	75
Appendix	79
About the Author	83

✜

PREFACE

The story is told that about ten years ago an ambitious young financial journalist, discussing his thoughts about financial assets with a senior associate, was handed by his elderly colleague a frayed, crudely-bound red volume and told that it might provide him with some extremely useful knowledge.[1] First published in 1841, the book deals with the mental processes of the masses that in numerous times in history gave rise to a huge boom in the prices of securities and land, only to be invariably followed (sometimes sooner, sometimes later) by a devastating catastrophe that, on some occasions, impoverished entire nations for a long period of years. Printed in London, its title was "Extraordinary Popular Delusions and the Madness of Crowds."

[1] Reprinted with permission of *The Economist Newspaper*, 1997.

In 1932, Bernard Baruch, one of America's most successful investors, wrote, after having read this book, what we all know (or at least should know)—that all economic movements, by their very nature, are motivated by crowd psychology. To this, I might add 'rather than by reasoned, sensible behavior.'

Although I did not know, until I read this book, the details of the Tulip Bulb mania of the 1620s, or of the Mississippi scheme of 1717 (when frenzied private investment drove up shares from 500 livres to 18,000, thence down to 300), or of the South Sea bubble of 1720 (when stock of the South Sea Company rose from £128 1/2 to £1,000 in just eight months) I have been quite aware of all economic depressions and panics in the U.S. since 1837, including the collapse of the Florida land boom of 1926. Thus it is that I see a number of disturbing parallels in today's financial markets. As the financial writer, Jim Rogers, has so aptly put it: "A market is at its worst when it looks like it is at its best; learn to question exultation, wait until despair is all around, then wait some more before you buy stocks."

For the record, let Baruch's additional and sagacious remarks be well remembered. "I have always thought that, if in the sorrowful era of the New Economics that ended with dizzily spiraling prices, we had all continually repeated that 'two and two still make four,' much of the evil might have been averted. Similarly, even in this time of gloom (1932), when many begin to wonder if declines will never halt, the appropriate abracadabra may be: 'They always did.'"

David Feldman

1925, AND AN EARLY LESSON IN FINANCE

My first exposure to the world of finance took place at the Shredded Wheat factory of the National Biscuit Company in the summer of 1925, when I was thirteen years old. Along with my parents and sister, we were on a tour of that facility. During the tour, the group ascended a stairway some 100 feet away from the plant that led to a ten-foot high platform which ahead and to the sides of us all we could see were what appeared to be huge round silos. At the guide's explanation that these silos (where the grain to be processed was kept in storage) held a total of one million bushels of wheat, my father's face turned white. He later explained that he held futures contracts at the time covering precisely one million bushels of wheat, being a firm and binding agreement to take delivery of that amount of wheat at a specified date in October and to make payment therefor. To him, one million bushels was a figure on a piece of paper—he had not the remotest idea, until that day when he saw those silos, of the physical magnitude of a million bushels of wheat. He later explained that his "long" position was such that if he did not liquidate it at some time prior to its expiration date, he might get a call from the railroad saying that they were loading twenty rail cars of wheat for him, "Where did he want it delivered?" (Movement of a futures price to a cash price is known as "convergence.")

But that wasn't the only lesson a thirteen-year-old boy learned that day. When told that wheat was currently selling at 52¢ a bushel, I quite naturally asked "But Dad, that's over a half-million dollars! Do we really have that kind of money?" "Not to worry, you don't need to pay for the wheat you buy until you sell the contracts—you need only to pay 10% now, and the rest you can borrow." Thus my first lesson in buying on margin.

A short time ago, I phoned the Production Manager at this same Nabisco plant, introduced myself to him and related this story. His first question to me was, "Are you still eating

Shredded Wheat?" I was embarrassed to tell him I never did, so I said, "Of course." Then he explained that now, some sixty-five years later, their storage silos are holding <u>forty-three</u> million bushels—not one million—and each silo stores not 20,000 but 60,000 bushels! It figures: in 1925 the population of the country was 114 million; today it is 266 million.

Seven years after that little episode in my life I graduated from Roger Babson's business school, then known as Babson Institute (now Babson College) and shortly thereafter took a job with a Wall Street firm, becoming one of its five partners two years later, remaining there in the capacity of "Statistician" (now called "Security Analyst") until I entered the Air Force shortly after the outbreak of the war in 1941.

A TOTALLY DIFFERENT COUNTRY

The social and economic changes that have taken place since the 1930s can scarcely be imagined by those who did not live through that period. My grandfather emigrated to the U.S. around the time of the Civil War. Like thousands of his compatriots, he was not especially happy with the idea of serving for five years in Franz Joseph's Austro-Hungarian army. And like the vast majority of them, he arrived on these shores with only the shirt on his back and without knowing a word of English. I am told that the accommodations on the ship were miserable and what little food there was was horrible. The first fully-powered steamship crossing of the Atlantic had taken place just twenty years previously. Against the possibility of a mechanical disaster, my grandfather's ship retained six masts. The voyage took exactly one month if all went as planned. Today there is but one passenger vessel on regular service on this route and it has been known to cover the same distance in a little over four days. But airline passengers flying the Concorde routinely have breakfast in Paris, lunch in New York and dinner in Los Angeles. In the 1930s just about everyone used the railroads for domestic travel, and a trip across the country needed five days and four nights. In 1926, Western Air Express, the forerunner of TWA, began flying passengers. In 1931, the total number of airline passengers on all U.S. airlines was 385,000; in 1996 nearly seventy million passengers passed through just one airport, Chicago's O'Hare. There was no Social Security, no Medicare, no miracle drugs but plenty of fatal diseases, no television, no VCRs and of course, no computers. Compared to the marvelous diagnostic procedures routinely realized today, one might say that medicine at that period of time was almost primitive.

THE BAD GUYS AND THE GOOD GUYS

Every profession has its share of scalawags. They carry on their nefarious, greedy activities not only to the detriment of the people they abuse but also to the vast majority whose dealings embody their probity and general decency.

One of the very first actions of the Roosevelt administration that was swept into power in the national election of 1932 was the establishment of the Securities & Exchange Act, passed by Congress in 1934. This law provided for a Securities and Exchange Commission whose function was to police the securities markets. It fulfilled a crying need at the time and was widely welcomed, even by those die-hards who had no use for the new president. What had been going on before this act was promulgated was so blatantly reprehensible that the vast majority of the public had lost all confidence in the financial institutions of the country.

Thus when I took a job with a brokerage firm in the early 1930s, I found scarcely any competition from other young college graduates for that type of position, so bad was the reputation of financial organizations in general. By far the great majority of young men of that period chose careers in marketing, manufacturing or accounting. As a result of the stock market crash of 1929 and the endless numbers of scams that typified that decade, the public was absorbed with the idea that most stock brokers were in essence manipulators and gamblers, sleazy people not to be trusted. This view was reinforced when Richard Whitney, the president of the New York Stock Exchange and a member of one of New York's oldest and most prominent families, went to prison for fraud, having been convicted of misappropriating the exchange's benefit fund. Was it any wonder that after the market crashed on October 29, 1929, ("Black Friday") after having reached on September 3 of that year the all-time high—up to then—in Dow Jones average of thirty industrial stocks—381.17—a crash that overnight wiped out twenty-six billion dollars' worth of investments—that the general public avoided stock brokers like the plague? Until their prices, too, dropped precipitously, bonds were the favored investment and for some odd reason, brokers who dealt exclusively in bonds were thought to cater to a higher class of person.

GAMES THE SWINDLERS PLAYED

Wall Street in the 1920s was famous for its corrupt "pools," whereby unsavory traders manipulated the prices of securities in such a way that the ordinary investor—usually a person of limited investment sophistication—would be left holding the bag. The stock market was the happy hunting ground of large numbers of professional speculators, in their heyday so well funded that they could move prices at will. In the ensuing three-year downturn in the markets, nearly all of these hot-shot operators lost everything they had ever owned. Among the best-known of this group was Jesse Livermore, who, in the summer of 1929, betting that the market would go down, went short; his prediction eventually proved to be correct but he was just a few months too soon and several years later, totally penniless, he committed suicide.

Also notorious in the '20s were the "bucket shops." The term originated from the bucket or basket kept in the offices of unscrupulous brokers into which were thrown the incoming orders of customers that were never executed, or if executed on the buying side, were then immediately sold. In other words, the broker was betting that the customer was always wrong, that an order to sell stock that he never actually purchased for the client was at a price that would have represented a loss if indeed he had bought the stock for the client in the first place. The broker would simply pocket the difference, the customer never suspecting that he had been taken. Since by far the majority of unsophisticated customers lost money "playing the market," as they used to say, the dishonest broker's gains would usually far outweigh any loss to him in those rare instances where the customer's "sell" order of a stock that he thought he owned (but actually never did) showed a paper profit. But later in the decade, when every dishwasher and shoeshine boy was a participant in the rapidly rising market, even the totally ignorant was making money for a time and so the diminishing chances of bucket shop profit greatly reduced their numbers.

Then there was the "financial speakeasy," of which, unfortunately, too many still exist today. The plan is simple: you first load up on some obscure stock, perhaps selling for pennies per share. Then you buy a "sucker list" of customers you plan to sell it to. Third, you need some method of communicating to the unsuspecting customers—a fancy little office with a bank of telephones plus of course, the mails. Finally, you put out and advertise a market letter, written on good paper and embellished with charts and color graphics, touting as an excellent buy the questionable shares the crook has purchased in large quantity for almost nothing. Since your firm is usually the only one making a market for these obscure shares, you then just sit back and watch the "buy" orders roll in. At one time in 1927 there were advertisements in the Wall Street district for hundreds of these well-written market letters, usually with high-sounding names. Subscription prices were low; often they were sent without cost to the subscriber. The objective of all, of course, was to unload stock to the gullible reader.

Of course, there are laws today against this sort of thing, but they are easily circumvented, all quite legally. I myself receive such a letter, or fancy brochure, nearly every month; it touts usually a mining stock or an oil stock that few have ever heard of, but there is a difference: at the bottom of the last page there will appear in type so small as to be scarcely legible these words or something similar: "The publisher (of this circular or letter) may or may not maintain a position in the shares of XYZ Corporation." If say 100 recipients of the circular read it, there will always be a certain number who never bother to read the fine print on the back page, nor may they even be able to read it. But the publisher has done his work well; he has complied with all applicable laws.

So it comes as no surprise that during the summer of 1929 the press carried headlines of all sorts of scams, of which the following, culled at random, are typical:

"Forged mortgages found in Brooklyn"

"Five guilty of hiding assets of 90-year-old clothespin concern"

"Brokers enjoined in fraud practice. Firm collected on stocks that were not purchased"

"Federal grand jury calls 20 employees of stock tipster sheet. Charged with using the mails to defraud by sending misinformation"

"Drive opens today on stock swindles. Prosecutor has list of 100 concerns. Tipster sheets that prey on the public, bucket shops and fake security deals to be the targets of Federal authorities"

"Broker is arrested in Chicago failure. Held on charges of embezzlement in 'Standard Oilshares' sales. Purchasers face a complete loss. $750,000 unaccounted for"

"Grand jury gets data on tipsters. Two men dealing in stocks of Avira Company and Coastal Airways, Inc., are being sought"

"380 stock tipsters accused by victims. Used mailing list of 13,000 names and a series of 'front men.' One, with a prison record, said to have made a million dollars in last three years"

A "NEW ERA" IS UPON US!

Further to this subject, it is interesting to read an editorial in the July 30, 1929, edition of *The New York Times* entitled "Cassandra of Kansas." It referred to an editorial by William Allen White, who was born in Emporia, Kansas, in 1868. He bought the *Emporia Gazette* in 1895 for $3,000 and turned it into the most respected small-town newspaper in the country. His autobiography, published in 1946, two years after his death, won a Pulitzer Prize. I quote from the *Times'* editorial:

> "'Hello, sucker' is the harsh manner in which *The Emporia Gazette* hails its fellow citizens these days—or at least those who drew their money out of the Emporia savings banks to put in on call on Wall Street at double interest rates or engaged in stock market speculation. 'You can't win,' admonishes the editor, and urges Kansans to go back to the grass-roots in this peroration:

If your son is playing the market and thinks it's smart, take an elm club to him. If your clerk is pouring his savings into the Wall Street rat-hole, look for another clerk. And if you are tempted to try the game yourself, just remember that Long Island and Greenwich highways are lined with limousines carrying big, fat plutocrats who thrive on the stream of money that comes from small-town hicks who think they can win a game in which they, have no chance.

Apparently, the *Gazette* visualizes dabbling in the market as exclusively a small-town temptation. Yet its remarks would readily be echoed by nearly every banker in New York City with the elision of only that vivid phrase about the limousine-lined roads. For New York bankers know what Kansas editors obviously do not, and this is that the only certain gainers from the volume of stock-market business are the brokers who get a commission on every purchase and sale. Since there are only a few thousand members of the New York Stock Exchange, it is clear that they could not line the roads as described. It is doubtless as bitter a reflection to a dweller in midtown Manhattan as to a citizen of Emporia that he has helped to buy those limousines and fatten the owners. And there are quite as many suckers in the Five Boroughs as among any equal number of human beings in the Middle West.

...When the wolves are ready for the shearing, fleece falls in the metropolis as well as on the windy plains of the Sunflower State. Speculation, unlike the tariff, is not a local issue."[2]

This *Times* editorial evokes, a day later, a letter to the editor from one E.E. Allen, of New Brunswick, New Jersey, which he headed "Concerning Cassandra." He wrote that "the *Times*' remarks on the *Emporia Gazette's* warning to would-be speculators contain much sound sense and it might be urged that The *Gazette's* admonition are logical and timely ...but you might have mentioned that any student of Greek mythology knows that Cassandra was endowed by the gods with the gift of prophecy but coupled therewith was the curse that she should never be believed."

What is really amazing about Mr. White's prediction of things to come and its complete agreement by the editor of *The New York Times* was that it was written just thirty-seven days before the Dow Jones Industrial Average reached its all-time high of 381.17 on September 3 and just three months before the greatest stock

[2] Copyright © 1929 by The New York Times Company. Reprinted with permission.

market crash in U.S. history. They were indeed a lone minority. All the "hot-shots," the "market gurus" and assorted "experts," with a precious few exceptions, were telling the country that the booming stock market would go on forever, that a "new era" was upon us, that old standards of security market valuations no longer had any meaning and that the accepted theory of business cycles had no validity any more. Forget the Dutch tulip bubble that bankrupted tens of thousands in 1637, forget the financial panic of 1873, when overexpansion of the railroads led to many railroad companies' insolvencies, forget the depression of 1893, brought about when the demand for steel rails on the part of the railroads dried up, forget the 1901 Northern Pacific Railroad panic, when the competition of two large Wall Street banking interests for control of that railroad created a corner in its stock, causing its price to rise to $1,000 a share, precipitating a general selling movement by brokers who were caught short and resulting in declines of 20% to 30% in the prices of most stocks in just a few hours of trading, forget the crisis of 1903 brought about by the huge issuance of IPOs of dubious companies with no record of past earnings, and forget the extremely violent market break of 1907, occasioned by the tying up of capital in company promotions and in speculation in the stock and commodity markets. Pay no attention, either, to the sweeping market declines of spring and fall 1920—only years earlier—caused by tying up immense sums of bank credit in merchandise bought at the high prices of the inflation months and the discovery, all of a sudden, that the stocks of goods that were piling up could not be sold. No, this now was a "new era" and henceforth there would be nothing to hold back, ever, the upward march of real estate, bank loans, stock prices and the general prosperity of the country.

Amid all the razzle dazzle, however, there were a few words of extreme caution. Roger Babson, the "Statistician" referred to earlier in this story, had this to say on September 5, 1929, fifty-five days before the bottom fell out of stock prices and distraught investors were getting urgent margin calls from their brokers began plunging to their deaths from high-rise buildings:

"Wise investors will begin paying off their loans and avoid margin speculation at this time because a crash of the stock market is inevitable... Sooner or later, the crash will take in the leading stocks and cause a decline of from 60 to 80 points in the Dow*. Fair weather cannot always continue; the economic cycle is in progress today, as it was in the past. Human nature has not changed—the crash that is coming may be terrific, (the market) will collapse like the Florida boom (of 1926)... there may be a stampede for selling that will exceed anything the Stock Exchange has ever witnessed because the number of declining stocks has steadily increased, which means that a great many people have lost money as well as made money."

Many people pooh-poohed this prediction because Babson had been saying essentially the same thing since 1927. However, on looking back, if investors had heeded his advice back then and refrained from jumping back in again, succumbing to the lure of ever-increasing prices, they would have ended up in 1932, at the bottom of the Great Depression, among the tiny few who, having retained their assets,

---

* Equivalent to 16% to 21%. The actual 30-month decline from the 1929 high was 89%.

were in a position to buy stocks that had lost, in some cases, 95% of their value in the previous thirty months and so could have made a killing when prices turned sharply upward after June of that year.

The Midland Bank, of Cleveland, in its bulletin of August 27, 1929, six days before the market reached a peak that it would not again see for twenty-five years, was an institution that shared Babson's dark views. It had things exactly right, namely:

> "614 of the stocks listed on the New York Stock Exchange, or more than 60% of all its listings, were lower on August 21st than on January 2nd and only 388 were higher during that period… prices have skyrocketed out of all reason and the market is in a dangerous position. Obviously, the market during 1929 has not been so rampantly bullish as some people suppose. On the contrary, it has been extremely selective. The blue chip stocks have gone forward rapidly on the basis of record-breaking earnings and excellent long-term outlook, but the bulk of the remaining stocks have been unable to do anything. In other words, the good stocks have been getting better while the poor stocks have been getting poorer, and as far as the number of stocks advancing or declining is concerned, one would be perfectly justified in saying that

the first eight months of 1929 have witnessed a bear market."

I am sure that those who were not alive during the 1930s do not have the slightest conception of the devastation resulting from the thirty-month stock market decline. To say that the market "dropped" is an understatement—it was just about obliterated! If you do not believe it, take a look at the following chapter showing the 1929 highs of a few stocks selected at random and compare them to the depression lows reached during the summer of 1932.

Dr. Irving Fisher, the most widely-respected economist of the pre-depression era, had this to say just fourteen days before the crash took the Dow Jones Industrials down a full 25% in just two sessions:

> "Stock prices have reached what looks like a permanently high plateau... I do not feel that there will soon, if ever, be a 50 or 60-point break. I expect to see the stock market a good deal higher within a few months than it is today... Through the influence of investment funds (read "mutual funds") the public is waking up to the superior attraction of stocks over bonds..."

Within ten weeks of his lecture before the Purchasing Agents Association it had gone down a full 48%—in the two sessions referred to above it lost 55 points. When Dr. Fisher's home in New Haven was about to be foreclosed, Yale University saved it for him by paying off his mortgage; he died in 1947 at the age of eighty.

1929 HIGHS VS. 1932 LOWS

There follows a tabulation of the 1929 highs for a number of stocks picked at random compared to their 1932, bottom of the depression, lows. They are typical of the more than 1,000 stocks listed on the exchange at that time. Still, they do not reflect what happened to Auburn Automobile, which, like many other stocks, reached its high of 514 <u>before</u> 1929; it dropped to the lowly price of 3 before it went to nothing after the auto manufacturer went bankrupt.

Stock	1929 high	1932 low
General Electric	403	8 1/2
Otis Elevator	450	9
Republic Steel	146 1/4	1 7/8
Warner Bros. Pictures	64 1/2	1/2
Johns-Manville	242 3/4	10
Spiegel-May-Stern	117 7/8	5/8

Nat'l Bellas Hess pfd.	118	1/8
Wabash Railroad	81 3/8	7/8
Int'l Combustion Engr.	103 1/2	1/2
R. H. Macy	255	17
Webster-Eisenlohr	113 3/8	5/8
Wright Aeronautical	149 1/2	3 7/8
Amer. Machine & Foundry	279 3/4	7 1/2
Chi., Rock Island & Pacific	143 1/2	1 1/2

✥

END OF THE YEAR 1929

OUR BUSINESS LEADERS PREDICT WHAT IS GOING TO HAPPEN IN 1930 AND BEYOND

As the year 1929 ended, a deep gloom had settled upon the nation. People didn't seem to know where to turn for some little measure of encouragement. They got it at the end of the year, when the leading bankers, businessmen and government officials gave the press their views of what lay ahead for 1930 and beyond. Almost to a man, they were highly optimistic. For instance, in Atlanta and the entire 6th Federal Reserve District "a consensus showed that the New Year would be more prosperous than for some time, with every indication of an excellent twelve months from a business and financial standpoint." As for the 8th District (St. Louis), "nothing in the nature of pessimism exists in our financial and industrial sections. Conditions are regarded as fundamentally sound, both in agriculture and in trade." From the Far West: "Representative businessmen who have checked up on the outlook for 1930 see nothing alarming on the business horizon. As regards the stock market, business leaders believe that only good can come out of the recent break." From Detroit: "Looking into the New Year, leaders of the automobile industry as a whole announce a clear view through virtually the entire year 1930. They were never more optimistic than at present." From New York: "Heads of leading public utilities are unanimous in expressing optimism for the continued prosperity of the country. It is expected that their expenditure for the year will exceed all records." And again from New York: "Bankers forecast gradual recovery. They say that the full year will prove sound. Loss of part of America's holdings should prove no worry. Business will not remain long in the doldrums—the full year will be a sound one. Authorities in all branches of finance and industry agree that already indications of improvement are seen, even in those lines that are depressed."

As for individual businessmen, the following remarks were typical:

"It is my humble judgment that we are witnessing today for the first time in American financial history what is really a panic, by which I mean a totally unnecessary, unreasonable and foolish display of mass psychology which has no reason in fact or reality. So far as human intelligence can comprehend, there is no reason for fear on the part of the American businessman or investor."

- From Harold Aron, Chairman, Exec. Comm.
International Germanic Trust Company

"Fortunately for business, the scars (of the stock market collapse) will be borne principally by individuals rather than by concerns and the economic balance of the nation is not appreciably disturbed. There are perfectly valid reasons for believing that the 12-month period (ahead) will round out a good year."

- Lewis E. Pierson, Chairman
Irving Trust Company

"I believe that 1930 will be one of the most soundly prosperous business years in American history."

- E.A. St. John, President
National Surety Company

"Any slackness that may be apparent in the general business situation can be attributed almost entirely to the hesitant state of mind in which business has been since the collapse of the stock market rather than to any important change in fundamental conditions. There can be little that may indicate a serious or continued depression."

- Frederick Ecker, President
Metropolitan Life Insurance Company

"Business is sound. The buying power of the country has been little impaired by the break in stock prices. A decline in security prices does not greatly affect the buying power of the community. The crash involved less than 4% of all the families in the nation or less than 1% of the total population."

- Dr. Julius Klein, Asst. Secretary of Commerce
Hoover Administration

My research has uncovered nearly fifty prophesies the country's leading businessmen, bankers and government officials contemplated as we slid into the worst economic calamity in the history of the United States. With the exception of a single one, every prediction of conditions in the cheerless year of 1930 was optimistic, even considerably upbeat. It makes one wonder if our leaders might say something for publication, but sadly their true feelings are quite the opposite. Most people want to be liked and the great majority are optimistic by nature. On the other hand, a pessimist, even when he or she has sound reasons for being pessimistic, is generally found to be unlikable, and so his or her thinking is disregarded most of the time. The expression "cold blooded verdict of the marketplace" has a great deal of truth. If you are going to invest in securities, set your emotions aside and keep them locked up somewhere to make sure that they do not interfere with your sound judgment. Not to do so has been the downfall of many an intelligent and otherwise successful investor.

✥

SO HOW COME A GROUP OF FOREIGNERS WERE THE ONLY ONES THAT HAD IT EXACTLY RIGHT?

I have made reference to one prophesy for 1930 that stands out from all the others because of its source, which was not American, and yet turned out to be 100% accurate. If one of our leaders had made such a statement he no doubt would have been berated as long as he lived by the vast majority, in their longing to hear only good news. Strangely, we'll never know who were the individuals whose shared opinions were so entirely accurate because *The New York Times*, in a small article in one corner of the financial page of their December 27, 1929, edition (datelined Berlin) referred to them only in the aggregate: "German financial circles." Here is the entire article:

> "Majority opinion in German financial circles looks for depression. They tend to believe that the Wall Street collapse foreshadowed a general

decline in trade and that stocks may enjoy big temporary recovery, but no prolonged bull movement is considered likely for several years to come."[3]

They hit it right on the button! A four-year recovery of some sort—about 30% in the DJIA—began after Roosevelt closed the banks and we went off the gold standard in the spring of 1933, and then a downtrend set in again. Where did they latch on to that crystal ball?

[3] Copyright © 1929 by The New York Times Company. Reprinted with permission.

ON BECOMING A STOCK BROKER
IN THE EARLY 1930s

In 1933, when I made the decision to become a stock broker, and considering the state of the economy at that time and particularly what had taken place in the years just prior to it, it was quite understandable that few young men had any desire to make that profession a career. And yet it was actually the very best time to enter the stock brokerage business provided that the firm could survive a few years of very limited commission revenue. After I was invited to become a partner of the firm at the beginning of 1936, it was a rather rare day when as many as 1,000,000 shares were traded on the New York Stock Exchange. There were many, many 400,000- and 500,000-share days and our firm needed a 1,000,000-share day to begin to make money from stock commissions—we did not engage in underwriting nor were we into commodities; we were a single-office Cincinnati firm known as a "wire house," telegraphing orders to our New York correspondent, who maintained a broker on the exchange floor who handled orders for our firm alone. But no one need have felt any pangs of sorrow for us because stock commissions were so meager. We had forty-two employees at the time and all our expenses were fully covered by the interest we received from those of our customers who had margin accounts. They could buy stocks with only 10% down and borrow the rest from us, their broker. We in turn borrowed from the bank at a rate of 1% or 2% less than the rate we charged the customer and we pocketed the difference. We still could not make any money but neither were we losing any; borrowing at 1 1/2% from the bank and loaning it out to the customer at 2 1/2%, or even 3 1/2%, depending upon the activity in the account, kept us going, while many brokerage firms that had few margin accounts couldn't withstand the low activity on the exchange and closed their doors. (Incidentally, the fact that one could buy stocks by putting down just 10% and borrowing the remaining 90% was a big factor in the crash of 1929, when brokers had to ask their customers to put up more money so as to protect their margin loans. If the customer was able to do that, his shares were thrown on the market by the broker and usually he was wiped out).

That brings me to the Securities Act of 1934, which established the Securities & Exchange Commission. It is fashionable with some people today to suggest that the government dispense with all regulations, since they are considered so onerous and so "bureaucratic." I must say, and most brokerage firms agree, that without the Securities Act of 1934 that was legislated into law under the sponsorship of Franklin D. Roosevelt, the financial markets would have forever been in the grip of complete chaos. The horrible things that took place in the 1920s and in previous decades would have continued to the point where the investment community would have lost all credibility. Everyone today concedes that the SEC is doing a fine job of policing the markets; the very first thing it did upon being established was to raise the margin requirements for buying stock; today they stand at 50%

instead of a mere 10% and that has had a great effect upon imparting relative stability to the financial markets. The regulations covering the issuance of financial reports and especially the initial public offerings of shares to the public, commonly referred to as "IPOs," have gone far to protect the investing public from unscrupulous brokers. *Business Week* magazine recently reported that they uncovered evidence that members of the New York Mafia have infiltrated Wall Street, apparently being the owners of several small brokerage firms. This has alerted the SEC, which doubtless will take whatever steps may be required. In any case, there is no evidence that such activities are anything other than very limited. On the other hand, no amount of legislation can deal with the greed and ignorance of any unsophisticated investor, looking upon the Exchange as nothing more than a big gambling parlor.

MAKING MONEY. EASIEST THING IN THE WORLD!

Now, in my eighty-sixth year of life, as I reflect upon my introduction to the stock brokerage business at the tender age of twenty-two, I cannot help but be impressed by how cocky I was to become at that time. Probably it would have been much better for me had I not had the misfortune to be so very successful right at the outset. I was hired by my employer as a "statistician," of which at the time there were fewer than 500 in the entire country (today there are some 23,000, in 70 regional groups). A "statistician" was later called "security analyst" and his only source of information about the companies whose securities he analyzed was the set of volumes of the Standard Statistics Company or Moody's, Poor's being an older publication but not as well known as the other two. Roger Babson, of course was a statistician and was greatly respected by the investment community, notwithstanding the fact that a majority of investors during the boom times did not follow his recommendations, much to their regret.

Even though many brokerage firms were unable to survive the depression years, when the volume of stock trading dwindled to almost nothing, it was actually the very best time to go into the business. That was because, as has been previously shown, stock prices were so very low that so long as a company did not go out of business, practically anything you might buy was certain to go up, if not sooner then later. I had actually been interested in the financial markets long before I started working and that experience proved most useful. My research had uncovered the fact that Reo Motors—the name comes from the initials of Ransom E. Olds, who founded the Oldsmobile, later acquired by General Motors—was planning to come out with a passenger car (they were making only trucks at the time) that required no gear shifting. Reo Motor Car shares were trading at around 1 1/2, less than 5% of its 1929 high; in those days the stock was paying $1.40 annual dividend. My instinct told me that when this marvelous invention was finally announced, Reo stock had nowhere to go but up. There was just one problem: at the low price of 1 1/2 I was unable to buy the stock on margin and in those dreadful times I didn't have the $175 (incl. commission) that I would need to buy 100 shares. Thus there was but one potential source of financing: my father, who, like nearly everyone else, had lost just about all his money during the long decline of the previous two-and-a-half years. I presented my case to him and he agreed that I might be onto something (or perhaps he merely wanted me to experience what it was like to be the holder of a very speculative stock). In any case, he did loan me the $175 and so I could now become a real stockholder.

Within just three weeks the shiftless car was definitely to become a reality, announced with great fanfare in the national press. Reo soared to 4 3/4! My $175 investment was then worth $475, a profit of 271% in three weeks, or 4,607% when annualized. That allowed me to pay off my father's loan and still end up with $300, which of course I did. Now, with all this newly-found wealth, it was natural that I should look around for another place to invest all that money. I found it very quickly: Bullard, a machine-tool manufacturer, whose stock was at 54 3/4 in 1929 (when it paid a $2.00 per share dividend) but was now available around 5, a price that would allow me to buy its shares on margin, which I promptly did. Right again! Within a matter of five weeks, it hit 9, where I sold it. I had been hoping to buy a typewriter with the profit. Now I could buy two typewriters and an adding machine!

When I went home at night—I was living with my parents—I could not help thinking, "For goodness sakes! How long has this been going on? Had no idea that it was so easy to make money!" And that was not only when I first became cocky—it was eventually to prove my downfall. I shall revert to this matter a little later in the story.

THE TYPICAL BROKERAGE OFFICE
OF THE 1930s

At this point in my saga I shall describe the typical brokerage office of the darkest days of the Great Depression of the '30s. Our firm was lucky enough to have a sufficient number of customer margin accounts, the interest on which fully covered our overhead. But, especially compared to a broker's overhead in this day and age, ours was remarkably low. Electric quotation boards were unknown back then and we didn't need to rent or invest in all kinds of high technology, also entirely unknown. Instead of an electric quotation board, one long wall of our boardroom was covered by a blackboard that extended from a foot-high platform up to about two feet from the ceiling, upon which were vertical yellow lines a quarter-inch wide and spaced about three inches apart. Running horizontally and intersecting these vertical lines some four or five inches below the top of the blackboard was another yellow line, from one corner of the wall to the other, above which was written the ticker symbol for around 200 of the most active stocks of the day. If a good customer, one who was an active trader, wanted the stock or stocks in which he happened to be interested listed as well on the board, we could comply with his wish by effacing some of the 200—everything was written with chalk— and substituting therefore the symbol or symbols of those stocks that were of interest to that particular customer. If his interest waned, we could then wipe off the latter and replace them with the original symbols. Upon this board, within each column, would be written the price of whatever stock was symbolized by its letter or letters at the top of the column, as recorded by the stock ticker located in the right hand corner of the boardroom, a few feet away from the blackboard. Three girls would read the one-inch-wide ticker tape coming out of the stock ticker; the one at the extreme right would tear off the tape, record on her third of the blackboard the price of any shares on the board that she watched over, and pass the tape along to the girl in the middle of the board, who did likewise before transferring the tape to the girl on the left. After the third girl had read the tape to note the symbols of the stocks under her jurisdiction and recorded the prices of those that were pertinent she simply tossed the tape into a waste receptacle near her and waited for the next piece of tape that would be handed to her by the girl in the middle third. A 500-million-share day on the New York Stock Exchange today is not too unusual; a 400,000 or 500,000-share session is a wholly different matter. We had a large number of those in the 1930s and in such instances the ticker tape could be completely without movement for several minutes, during which time the three girls would just stand around without anything to do. Conversely, if there were a few million shares traded, they would be very hard-pressed to keep up with the tape, but none ever appeared to be rattled. Whatever tension they may have felt, they managed to suppress it because in those days, when grown men with families to support were reduced to selling apples on street corners, any job, no matter how little it may have paid, was considered precious. If on those rare occasions when one of the girls was obliged to visit the ladies' room on a very busy day, she could send a signal to one of the bookkeepers in the back office, who would rush out to relieve her for a few minutes.

Using a blackboard to record stock prices was indeed crude compared to the electric quotation boards that have been in use now for several decades, but the system had one decided advantage. Whereas the electric board usually shows only the day's current price and the high and low thus far during that day, prices recorded by chalk in a column on a blackboard reveal every single transaction that has taken place, and in an orderly fashion; thus while the electric board may show the latest price, say 35, off a particular stock, handwritten recordings show the entire trend—how it arrived at 35—for example 33 3/4, 33 7/8, 33 1/2, 33 3/4, 34, 34 1/8, 34 1/4, 34 3/8, 34 5/8, 34 3/4, then 35.

1932—BOTTOM OF THE BARREL
JUST COULDN'T BE WORSE

For their services the boardroom girls were paid a weekly salary of $25, not great by any reckoning, but quite adequate during those times and a figure that certainly permitted no luxuries but allowed a single girl to maintain a small apartment and have enough left over to buy the necessities of life, among them a loaf of bread for 10¢, a newspaper for 3¢, a postage stamp for 2¢. The average price of a medium-sized brick home in Cincinnati was $6,000; a gallon of gasoline was at times as low as 8¢. "Lunch out," that is, in a restaurant, could run from 80¢ to $1 and a cup of coffee was 5¢. In 1935 a dollar was a real dollar—today you would need $1,233 to be able to buy what $100 could buy during that year. Until Roosevelt took us off the gold standard in 1933, an ounce of gold was worth $20.67; now that same ounce will cost you $350.00. In the depths of the depression girls in sweatshops sometimes worked from eighty-one to eighty-five hours a week; throughout Massachusetts the pay for such work was 5¢ per hour. One clothing sweatshop in the western part of that state was found to be paying 1¢ per hour! In New York State, canneries paid 8¢ per hour to women and 10¢ to men. None was ever known to pay more than 22¢. Children under sixteen in the textile and clothing industries received a median of $3.10 a week and women $6.58, but in New Jersey there were women who worked for as little as $1.50 a week—that's $78 for a whole year's work! Many girls were paid $1 a week as "learners," even though they may have been operating for five or six years. In South Carolina's cotton mills, the eleven-hour night shift—fifty-five hours per week—paid $8.25 per week. And the Supreme Court ruled that a minimum wage was unconstitutional! Then there's the story of the Chamber of Commerce of a small town in Pennsylvania that gave $1,000 and free rent, light and heat to a luggage manufacturer to get it to establish itself there. After seven weeks, the company absconded without having paid a single cent of wages to its employees. Another Chamber of Commerce paid a shirt company $2,500 to induce it to move its factory to its town. The wages were around $3 per week. After three months the company moved its factory to another town for another $2,500 and paid the same low rate of wages.

By the end of 1933, more than 5,000 banks, with deposits of three billion dollars, had failed; but in Canada there was not one single bank failure and just twenty-six since 1876. By 1933 farm prices had fallen 56% below their average level of 1929. That's when Roosevelt's New Deal began a program to require farmers to plow under every third row of corn and to dump some commodities into the ocean in order to raise prices, with inconsequential results. In 1930 the gross public debt of the U.S. government was $16,185,000,000, equivalent to $131.51 per capita. In 1996 it was $5,217,305,000,000 (five trillion two hundred seventeen billion three hundred and five million), or $19,681.26 per capita. The gross domestic product in 1940 was $906,000,000,000—in 1995 it was $7,245,000,000,000. The gross public debt at this time is 64% of the gross domestic product—in France and in the United Kingdom it is 57.6%, in Germany, 61.6%, in Italy 123% and in Belgium a whopping 133%. But in the Netherlands it is only 79%.

Some people have the rather naive idea that a 2 1/2% annual rate of inflation is benign—"inflation is under control." Actually, 2 1/2% is horrendous! Compounded over a period of ten years, it results in a 28% cost-of-living increase. At 3% a year, prices in ten years will rise by 35! Nothing benign about either rate.

The year 1932 marked the very bottom of the Great Depression, but it was to last through the entire decade. Only after war broke out in Europe late in 1939 did our factories return to some degree of normalcy, spurred by the production of military goods. Except for a rather strong upward trend that began in late 1929 and lasted about three months, the prices of shares on the stock exchange went almost straight down until June 6, 1932, when the Dow Jones Industrial Average reached its bottom of 41.22. From that point forward and for the next seven years there was, with interruptions, a slight upward trend, which suddenly stalled at the end of 1937. At the end of the decade the DJIA stood at about 150, still less than 40%

of the 1929 peak of 381.17, which it was not to see again for another fifteen and one half years.

Those were very difficult years for brokerage firms; many merged with others or simply went out of business. Our firm was no exception. Although I had brought it a number of new customers, whose accounts I managed, not many were the type that traded and generated commissions. In addition, we had fewer margin accounts due to deaths and a general reluctance upon the part of investors to take on debt. This was reflected in the price of a seat (membership) on the New York Stock Exchange. One sold in 1938 at $157,000 but shortly thereafter changed hands at just $17,000, its all-time low. The persistent low trading activity was having its toll.

We had, fortunately, excellent relations with all of our forty-two employees. The office atmosphere was always very relaxed. Employee turnover was just about non-existent. Even the senior partner was addressed by his first name, as the other four, including me, always were. The staff was aware of the fact that the firm had lost money for several years and the general gloom no doubt was producing a certain amount of nervousness. Thus the partners were quite surprised when on March 9, 1938, the senior partner, upon entering his office, found on his desk an envelope addressed to the firm, which, opened, revealed this letter:

> "A meeting of all the employees was held yesterday at 3:15. At this time a very thorough discussion was had relative to general business conditions and the fine treatment which we have received as the employees of this firm.
>
> A motion was made and unanimously passed that this letter be written to you thanking you for all past favors shown to us, together with the recommendation that you take steps to make satisfactory cuts in our salaries, effective March 15th, 1938, which will in some way help to reduce the extreme overhead expense.
>
> We pledge to you our loyal support and assure you that we will do everything in our power to save money, and also to obtain any possible business that might help to increase the firm's revenue. May we also reaffirm our confidence in the abilities of the partners of the firm."

As I look back upon this episode, coming as it did out of the blue, I am impressed by how it exemplified the spirit of those depressing times. During the worst of the depression, very rare indeed was a family that possessed any liquid assets. Cash was king—if you happened to have any, you were really in the driver's seat. Everyone in the country seemed to be in the same boat—a very leaky one—and everyone helped his neighbor as best he could. How very different from the relationship today between most companies and their employees!

"BRING BEER BACK WITH FRANK AND JACK"

"Bring Beer Back With Frank and Jack!"
That was the rallying cry of the Democratic Party during the presidential campaign of 1932. Things were so bad one simply had a hard time believing that they could get any worse. Thousands of veterans had come to Washington, pitched their tents on the Mall or wherever there was room to do so, and demanded that President Herbert Hoover authorize the payment of a bonus to them. In response, Hoover called out the Army, under the command of General MacArthur, who had threatened to send tanks in to destroy the tents along with whatever meager possessions they sheltered. So bringing back the matter of alcoholic drinks, which had been prohibited in this country since the 18th Amendment to the Constitution was passed in 1920, not only added a little spice to the campaign but was something that just about all

the electorate favored. The amendment was the result of Congress' passage, the year before, of the Volstead Act, sponsored by Senator Andrew Volstead of Minnesota, which provided for the enforcement of a law that banned "the manufacture, sale and transportation of all types of alcoholic beverages," thereby causing the unanticipated effect of turning the business over to the "bootleggers"—gangsters and murderers of whom Al Capone is probably the best-known. "Frank and Jack," of course, referred to Governor Franklin D. Roosevelt of New York, who was running against President Hoover, and his chosen running mate, John Nance Garner of Texas, who was the Speaker of the House of Representatives, known to everyone as "Cactus Jack." (He was a conservative Democrat who later broke with President Roosevelt.)

The subsequent election swamped the Republicans, who carried just two states—Maine and Vermont. The popular vote was 22,821,857 for Roosevelt and 15,761,841 for Hoover (472 Electoral College votes for Roosevelt and only 59 for Hoover); there were also 884,781 for Norman Thomas, the perennial candidate of the Socialist Party.

All of this was not lost upon a young man who had just made what he considered a "killing" in the stock market and who kept thinking that if it was so easy, it had to be because he was so smart. Will the newly-elected administration go ahead now and try to get the Volstead Act repealed? Certainly worth a gamble—who was against it besides the Women's Christian Temperance Union, with their 250,000 members, those misled ladies who believed that they could improve public morals through abstinence from alcoholic beverages? If that really were to happen, the stock of any company that was making alcohol would really take off!

So the security analyst did a little research and came upon the American Commercial Alcohol Company, whose stock could be picked up around $14 a share. I transmitted my findings to those of my customers whose accounts I was managing and nearly all of them agreed that it looked like a terrific speculation. So I began to buy for them and for myself as well, margining my purchases with 10% down and borrowing the rest. The stock soon began to move up, with the result that each time it did, I added to my holdings, ending up with 1,400 shares, which were fully margined. My equity was now some $40,000! Imagine that! And only a few months earlier, I had borrowed the munificent sum of $175, which started it all!

Some of my customers were getting nervous, so high now was the stock, and sold so as to protect their profits. For many years, my father had been trading in commodities, as well as stocks, and had lived through the wild 1920s and the dreadful 1930s and he begged me to dispose of all my American Commercial Alcohol shares at the market and without further delay, adding that the speculative fever in the alcohol stocks had reached such a ridiculous level that a crash was certain to be close at hand. That advice was given to me on July 13, 1933, a date that I shall never forget because of how it was received by me. Even though I had always respected my father's opinions of events to come, in the back of my mind was how very talented I was to have turned, in just a matter of months, that measly $175 into $40,000, even though it was "on paper." How could I possibly lose? No, I could not possibly sell, because the stock was sure to hit

100, the magic number, not 99 1/8, 99 1/2, but 100!

A week later, July 20, American Commercial Alcohol closed at 89 7/8. For apparently no reason at all, the following day the alcohol stocks were deluged with "sell" orders that came in from all over the country. After the first hour of trading, my stock had not even opened, so great was the spread between the highest bid and the lowest offer. Nor had any transaction taken place by the end of the second hour, nor even the third. Finally, at 2 P.M., a huge block of its shares appeared on the ticker tape at 50, down 39 3/4 points! At long last, buyers and sellers had been able to agree on a price. And I was financially ruined from one day to the next! In fact, the collapse had come so fast that there had not been even any time for the firm to sell my shares so as to cover my loan, and now I was indebted to it for some $17,000, a sum I had no possibility to come up with, since at the time my only asset was my partnership interest in the firm and we had been losing money right along.

So far as I was concerned, it was a panic situation, made even worse by my father's fulminating against me for my having disregarded the advice given me by one who, during the course of his life, had lived through more than one enervating experience. But what to do now? "Only one thing to do," was the answer. "I will guarantee your account with the firm (he had an account there as well, but abstained from wild speculations) and then I will buy for your account 500 shares of Allis-Chalmers Manufacturing stock, worth enough to cover what you owe them. You'll still end up with absolutely nothing, but at least you'll be off the hook. You can expect a tongue-lashing from your partners but since you've brought them a lot of business since you started to work there and have handled the accounts quite well, it's unlikely that they're going to fire you. Allis-Chalmers (a manufacturer of farm machinery) is a bargain at its current price and is sure to go up over time; you can sell it then to pay off the loan and you might even end up with a little equity, but if and when you do, don't ever again do such foolish things and, by all means, listen to people who know more than you do."

This sobering experience abruptly put an end to whatever amount of self-importance I had possessed after that original purchase of those unloved Reo Motor Car shares. Looking back on it all, I have to say that when it came to investing, my father made some horrible mistakes, but the fact is that he was right more often than he was wrong and in the final analysis, that's all that matters. The Allis-Chalmers shares that he had purchased for me behaved precisely as he had predicted. Little by little, their price moved upward until finally I was in a position to pay off the debit balance in my account and have a little real money left over, to do with as I pleased. But unfortunately my father, a heavy smoker, passed away very suddenly and never lived to see the outcome of the love and caring he had bestowed upon his son.

ON THE WAY TO BECOMING A MILLIONAIRE! THE LOFT, INCORPORATED, FROLIC

What followed next is another story of triumph and sheer ordeal, as well as a valuable lesson that I have never forgotten, to my everlasting well-being.

It so happens that in the late 1930s a nearly bankrupt candy retailer, with numerous stores in the New York area, instituted a lawsuit against a certain Mr. Guth, its president, who, according to the company, stole from it the sum of $9,000, which he used to buy a 91% interest in a firm called Pepsi-Cola, that dated back to 1885. Getting its $9,000 back from Guth was not the purpose of the lawsuit; it claimed that his investment, made many years earlier with the company's stolen money and now worth $31 million, belonged to Loft and not to Mr. Guth.

Upon learning of this, I could see right away that here was one of those rare speculative opportunities that presents itself only once in a lifetime! If you bought Loft shares at the prevailing price of $1.25 and if it lost the lawsuit, you would still own the shares of a company close to bankruptcy but you would know that your loss could never exceed $1.25. On the other hand, if Loft won the suit it would immediately come into shares worth $31 million and of course its stock would soar.

I brought this to the attention of our customer's men—now known as "registered representatives" and to a man they agreed that Loft stock was certainly a worthwhile speculative "buy." Fortunately, the stock was actively traded and we were able to pick up many thousands of shares for our customers. I latched on to 2,000 at prices between 1 1/8 and 1 3/8. But as in every instance, it was not all clear sailing, because a lawsuit can drag on for years, and indeed this one did. Some of the early buyers bailed out, but I not only held onto mine but considered buying more when the price sank to 3/4¢, a 35% paper loss. I discussed the matter with the customer's men—their disillusionment was rather widespread, their typical position being that when so many "good" stocks were available at such low prices, why pour money into a "dog" like Loft, which was still teetering on the edge of bankruptcy? Well, my father always preached the virtue of patience; after all, the reason for buying the stock a couple of years earlier was still valid, so why not pick up more for next to nothing? That's what I did, and by the time in 1939 that I had taken a trip down to Dover, Delaware, where the trial was being held, in an effort to pick up what information I could, I was the holder of the stock of just one company—Loft, Inc.—to the extent of 8,000 shares for which I had paid an average price of 1 1/2, an investment of $12,000 and one that I owned outright—no margin to worry about.

Not long afterward, it happened! After three years, Loft won its lawsuit against Mr. Guth! It promptly came into $31 million and of course the stock sky-rocketed! For every point it went up, I was $8,000 richer—a lot of money indeed in those depressing times. Beyond that, I was now the fair-haired boy wonder—I stuck it out while scarcely anyone else had!

Joy, however, was short-lived. There's always something to spoil the party. Loft had hit $8 and the profit of my $12,000 investment was now $52,000! Within a mere thirty days, the news ticker carried the story that Coca-Cola had entered a lawsuit against Pepsi-Cola, claiming that the latter had no legal right to use the word "cola." The moment that news became public, I was hit with a single idea: how could any company prevail over that giant, Coca-Cola, with their high-priced lawyers? Better to sell now to protect that huge profit, still only on paper. But wait a second; if that's sure to happen, why not also make money from the fall that's bound to come? Sheer greed, but the conjecture seemed so appealing. "Do it right now, while you still have the chance!" So, after having held onto Loft through thick and thin for more than three years, I handed our telegrapher an order to sell 16,000 shares—the 8,000 I owned and a second 8,000 "short." It wasn't thirty seconds before the ticker tape reported a sale, reading like this: "8000.8000." Quite obviously, it had to be mine. The speed with which someone had taken my 16,000-share order set off almost a cold sweat in me. For those quiet days, that was a lot of stock; did somebody know more than I did? As it turned out, this spur-of-the-moment decision had two unhappy consequences. It nipped right in the bud my chance to become a millionaire and it just about wiped out the $52,000 I had already made from a three-year stock holding!

Evidently no one else became especially upset because big Coke was about to sue upstart Pepsi. Loft dropped a fraction on the news, but rallied later in the day to a new high for the year, not far from its all-time high of 11 1/2, reached April 1, 1929. Now the shoe was on the other foot! Every point that it rallied left me out-of-pocket by $8,000! And it wouldn't stay down—the following week it easily surpassed the old high. In speculation, there's nothing worse than being short when your stock is going up. After all, when you're "long" you know how much you can lose: 100% of what you've invested. But when you're short, the sky's the limit, because at some point you must buy back, at whatever the going price may be, an equal number of the shares you sold, but only borrowed from a third party, in order to pay back the party who loaned you the stock you were determined to sell because you considered it over-priced.

As it turned out, the court eventually ruled that Coca-Cola had no right to be the exclusive owner of the word "cola." The cola is an African tree whose nut contains caffeine; therefore the word may be used in a generic manner. So it was with perfectly good reason that Loft kept going up. At 12 1/2, I had had enough—I could no longer stand it, and so bought at the market price 8,000 shares in order to close out this unhappy transaction. At the end, I was left with a $12,000 profit on my original investment. Not bad, actually, but just a small fraction of that $52,000 I once had—on paper.

That purchase, as it happened, was a blessing in disguise. Over the following two years, the stock of Pepsi-Cola Company, now spun off to Loft's shareholders, reached $125 a share and didn't even stop there. With all its splits, the stock today is worth several times that. But so what? Even if I had not gone short, it was highly unlikely considering that I was a short-term trader, that I would have held my original shares much beyond $15. I most certainly would have succumbed to the lure of a huge short-term profit; in fact, might have sold it even below $15, a figure that would have gotten me out with $120,000.

One thing that this experience taught me was that, in investing, you should never cry over spilt milk, never look back, because if you're going to do that you might very easily drive yourself crazy. Valuable lessons can be uncovered from past events, but only the future is of importance.

I recall another incident, a few years into the 1920s, that in one respect has a striking similarity to my Loft story:

Our firm's stock clearing was handled in New York by our correspondent in that city, Frazier Jelke & Company. The Jelke family, after Unilever, was the country's largest producer of oleomargarine. The head of the family, Frazier, was a very wealthy man and had a seat on the New York Stock Exchange. However, he had a reputation of being quite a playboy and left the management of his Wall Street firm to others, among them a well-dressed Spanish gentleman by the name of Señor Cassanova. The latter's big clients included another man with a Spanish background by the name of Sosthenes Behn. Behn was the head of the Porto Rico Telephone Company, which later became the huge conglomerate, International Telephone & Telegraph Company. Jelke traveled only in high society and was greatly impressed by big names. Eventually he lunched with Mr. Behn, who regaled him with what a wonderful firm the telephone company was and how outstanding were its future prospects. So bedazzled was Mr. Jelke by all this sweet talk that he promptly instructed his office to buy 50,000 shares of the telephone company's stock, which was selling at the time for more than $100 per share. Since it had sold as high as 149 1/4 earlier that year, he probably thought he was getting a bargain, although his firm's statistician had expressed some doubts as to the wisdom of the purchase. He carried the stock all the way down to $15 and then to $5. How very clever of him to sell at that point! On May 28, 1932, it sold as low as 2 5/8, the all-time bottom. The long ride down from over $100 to less than 3 had given him a huge tax deduction, which he made use of for many years that followed his recklessness.

If there may be a moral to these two experiences, it is that, in investing, impulsiveness often turns out to be the kiss of death. Making money has never been an effortless task; above all, it calls for a well-thought-out plan and that involves a degree of time. When the plan is abandoned from one moment to the next, for whatever reason, disaster very often follows. Impulsiveness is one thing, bad judgment quite another. I am reminded of a story that one of my New York associates always liked to tell: in 1926 he bought an Overland Six automobile—the predecessor of today's Jeep. To get the funds to do so, he was obliged to sell the few shares he owned in a company called Computing-Tabulating-Recording. Although he had paid just a few hundred dollars for his shiny new Overland, it had really cost him more than a million. That's because Computing-Tabulating-Recording, which at one time had been a producer of meat-slicing machines, later became known as International Business Machines Corporation and that would have been the value of his few shares shortly before he died.

✣

AND WHAT ABOUT TODAY'S MARKETS?

In today's stock market environment, two axioms get a great deal of undeserved attention, both of which are, in my opinion, completely false. One is "Buy only for the long pull." The other is "Never try to time the market." To an infinitesimal degree there may be some validity to this kind of advice. "Buy only for the long pull" is really a cop-out, an insurance policy. When that advice is followed by a market meltdown, the person who gave it will always be able to fall back on the standard excuse—"Don't blame me if you've lost a lot of money, I advised you to buy for the long pull." What is never broached, of course, is that "the long pull"—whatever it means—can be as much as twenty-five years! That's how long it took after the market crashed in 1929 to recover to its old high of 381.17. And if one goes back over the history of the Dow Jones averages since 1896, it becomes obvious that after several stock market peaks since that time, enough were followed by long down-trends that tried the patience of all but the most steely-nerved investor. As for "timing the market," the same guru who cautions against doing that thinks that security comes by buying mutual funds, not realizing that the managers of such are in every sense doing exactly that! Don't they try to look good knocking their brains out every three months to show how smart they were to outshine the S&P 500? If that isn't timing, what would you call it? They engage in another practice that, while not strictly illegal, is certainly unethical. Just prior to the end of a quarter, when they must make their portfolio public, they will buy some stocks that have exhibited a spectacular rise during the preceding three months, while selling the "dogs" that have declined in price or at best done nothing. That can't change their three-month record, of course, but doesn't it make their quarterly report look so much prettier? And while on this subject, do most people who own mutual funds realize how many times the managers of those funds are changed? Sometimes it's like a revolving door; very few, indeed, are those funds that have been guided by the same manager over a period of years. When results don't measure up, when the constant pressure to outshine the S&P 500 has had no happy conclusion, out goes the hapless manager to look for another job, even in those cases where time would have proven him absolutely correct!

It is natural for everyone, in and out of finance, to try to predict the future. That is a thankless job, because there is always the chance that something will come up—some catastrophic event—that no one had anticipated. It could be a huge political upheaval, a disastrous earthquake or hurricane that could cost billions or even an economic depression. So when the so-called "experts" spout forth their claim of being the fountainhead of all knowledge, listen politely but don't make the mistake of taking them too seriously.

APPENDIX

Like everyone else, I have had my ups and downs in life, but the ups were always much longer than the downs, which somehow I have managed to survive. But it would be a mistake to say that I am an optimist where the future is concerned. I believe that this country has some core problems that can be solved only with an amount of discipline that I do not see the American people as having. Just mention raising the gasoline tax even a measly 5¢ per gallon to help pay for our deteriorating highways and bridges, and all hell breaks loose! The annual budget deficit of the U.S. government cannot possibly be eradicated until those self-serving politicians address the problem of entitlements, something no one has yet had the courage to do. And how much longer will the young people today continue to pour out a good chunk of their earnings to support a fast-growing population of old people like myself? They should not and they will not allow vast sums of money to be transferred to the very people who caused them a big part of their problems. I've heard old people express intense objections to PACs and to lobbyists, but these same people think it's quite all right to support the AARP, as if a $5 yearly fee for each of their 33 million members weren't enough—after all, that's just $165 million annually to lobby Congress. It was raised 60% not so long ago, so that now they have $264 million at their disposal every year! It simply staggers the imagination! And it is wrong, dead wrong!

At eighty-five, the only advice I can give to those who are coming up is to keep yourself as well informed of everyday events as you possibly can. Listen to the advice of others. There is always something to be learned. But when the chips are down and decisions are to be made, your own ideas should play as big a part, if not more of a part, than those of others. If mistakes are to be made, as surely sometimes they will be, they will at least have been your mistakes and there will always be a hope that you can find profit in that.

ABOUT THE AUTHOR

David Feldman's first exposure to investing was in 1925 at the tender age of thirteen. Mr. Feldman observed firsthand the madness of mass psychology that fueled the greatest stock market crash in history in 1929. He was a partner of a New York Stock Exchange firm during the darkest days of the Great Depression of the 1930s and into the 40s. He later spent many years in Eastern Europe as an international trade consultant and specialized in the financing of natural gas and petroleum exploration activities. Since 1979, the author has specialized in environmental problems, including consulting services relative to the reduction of the solid waste stream. He has spoken before numerous meetings of environmental officials of counties and municipalities and is active in the state legislatures lobbying for the legislation banning the incineration of municipal solid waste.

He graduated from Babson Institute of Business Administration in 1932, and the New York Stock Exchange Institute in 1936.

Mr. Feldman now in his eighties, currently lectures around the country, describing what he sees as a frightening parallel in the financial markets of the 1990s to the misguided euphoria of 1929.